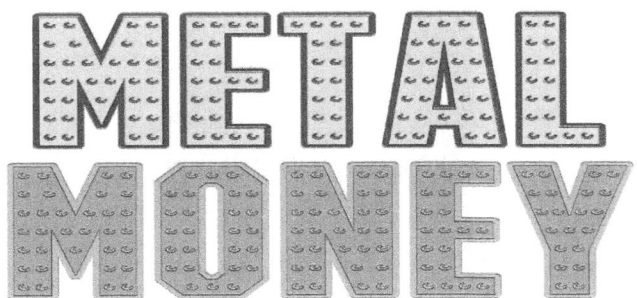

HOW TO EASILY EARN THOUSANDS IN YOUR SPARE TIME SCRAPPING METAL!

MIKE MCLEAN

AUTHOR MIKE MCLEAN

Check out my books on how to make money
in Section 8 rental properties!

www.section8bible.com

<u>Other books by this author:</u>
Section 8 Bible: How to Invest in Low-Income Housing
Section 8 Bible Volume 2
Section 8 Bible Volume 3
Section 8 Secrets: Get Housing Assistance Faster

ISBN: 978-0-9801759-5-0

Metal Money
Copyright 2019 by Michael McLean / McLean Co.
All rights reserved.

TABLE OF CONTENTS

Chapter 1: The Preface 1
Chapter 2: The Introduction 3
Chapter 3: I Was a Metal Moron! 7
Chapter 4: The Early Bird Catches the Worm 17
Chapter 5: More Homes, More Metal! 23
Chapter 6: I Caught a Brake, I meant Break 27
Chapter 7: Getting the Word Out 31
Chapter 8: Thinking Outside the Metal Box 37
Chapter 9: Dumpster Diving 45
Chapter 10: Holiday Scrap 51
Chapter 11: School's Out! 55
Chapter 12: Learn the Trash Route 57
Chapter 13: Scrap Metal House Calls 63
Chapter 14: To Separate or Not to Separate That is the Question! ... 67
Chapter 15: Picking off of the Pile 71
Chapter 16: Tools Needed for Picking off the Pile 77
Chapter 17: Hospital Hospitality 83
Chapter 18: Apartment Complexes 87
Chapter 19: Yes, You Can-Can 91
Chapter 20: Building a Good Route 99
Chapter 21: What You Will Need to get Started 101
Chapter 22: Craigslist – Let Go – Marketplace 107
Chapter 23: Mike's Final Thought's 109
Chapter 24: Wrapping it Up! 113

CHAPTER 1
THE PREFACE

Just like the cover of this book says, I'm going to show you how to *easily* make an extra $2,000 bucks a month, picking up scrap metal in your *spare* time. I'm not telling you to quit your fulltime job, or the minute you get home from work to go out hunting for metal for six or eight hours a night, nope! I'm going to tell you exactly where to find scrap metal and how to have people call you and tell you to, "Come and get it," almost as if they were ringing a dinner bell!

Take a look around, almost everything is made out of some form of metal. Which is good because the U.S. dollar is also backed up by some form of precious metal. Steel, brass, aluminum, copper, silver, gold, etc., every single form of metal is worth money and every day, people walk right past it, throw it away, or even worse, **pay** someone else to get rid of it for them! I myself was one of "those guys." That was until I came to my senses and wised up.

By the time that you finish this book, you're going to know exactly how to find scrap metal and make a nice buck every month without killing yourself, that I guarantee. So, if you like free money, you're gonna love this book!

CHAPTER 2

THE INTRODUCTION

My name is Mike McLean and I am a multi-millionaire! Not from scrap metal, I'll get back to scrap in a minute. I made my fortune in the real estate business. Not your typical high end, commercial real estate and not even apartment complexes. No, I made my millions in low end, gritty, grimy, bottom feeder, Southwest Philadelphia rowhomes/section 8 homes, and I still do. At my high point, my partner and I owned over 300 homes and we sold them all off during the real estate boom in 2005, instantly becoming millionaires!

I sat on the sidelines for a couple of years and after the market crashed in 2008, I made another move and jumped back into the game again. Once again we acquired over 200 homes, it's all about timing folks! If you want to check my credentials to make sure you're not reading the writings and ramblings of a bullshitter, you can go to my website @www.section8bible. com or just search Section 8 Bible on YouTube or Amazon and you'll see my landlord video's and books, go ahead, I'll wait here.

See, I told ya. I wasn't born with the silver spoon in my mouth and I took one $10,000 rowhome and turned it into a Section 8 real estate empire! Today, I sell a series of books for landlords and I own and operate over 250 Section 8 homes in Southwest Philadelphia. By now, you've got to be asking yourself, "we'll what the hell does this have to do with scrap metal?" I'm going to get into that and this whole thing is going to gel together quite nicely, I promise.

I'm going to end the introduction with this and then we're going to dive into showing you how to literally pick up some extra money every month for the rest of your life. Okay, when I do something, I do it right! Whether it's crunching numbers and knowing the precise time to pull the trigger on a $500,000 package deal of investment properties or something not as big, like knowing the exact time and place to go out and pick up a ton of scrap metal. To me, money is money and I'm all about making it. The money that I make in real estate is not any greener than the money that I make from scrap metal. Even know this book is about how to pick up some spare money every month, I will write it and treat it just as importantly as my real estate books, that, I also guarantee! Hey, you're reaching into your pocket to purchase *my* book so I'm going to give *you* everything that I've got! One thing that I'm not going to do is use big, fancy words and act like I'm the smartest guy in the room because I'm not. Look, I made my fortune in Section 8 homes, I didn't go to college, my favorite subject in high school was lunch, and I scrap metal. How smart can I be? This I will tell you, I'm smart enough to make a buck and I've been that way all of my life. I may not be Bill Gates rich but I get up and go to work every day so I'm not broke. By the time that you put this book down, you'll also know how to make a buck and the how and when to find scrap metal. Now let's go get it!

CHAPTER 3

I WAS A METAL MORON!

Alright, this is how it all got started. In 1997, my business partner and I started buying cheap, Southwest Philly rowhomes. We'd buy them very cheap, say ten to fifteen thousand, and rent them out to a section 8 tenant.

This is what a Southwest Philly rowhome looks like.

When we'd purchase these homes, they were always loaded up with junk. We'd purchase the properties in "as is" condition which means the seller could leave the property in any condition that they wanted to, and we would buy it. So naturally, they'd take all their valuable possessions and leave the bullshit, and for about a year, that's exactly what I thought it was, bullshit!

We'd pull our trucks up to the house and begin cleaning it out. We'd throw everything onto our trucks and take it straight to the dump. The dump would weigh our trash and charge us $75 bucks per ton to get rid of our "trash."

The Dump!

Beds, carpets, stoves, furniture, refrigerator, dishwashers, toys, clothes, washers, dryers, etc., everything that was in the house went to the dump. Listen, I'm a cheap bastard and I'd bitch and moan all the way back to the property. What was I bitching about? That I just paid anywhere from $75 to $150 bucks to get rid of trash and half of it was metal, what an idiot I was!

Metal toys

washer and dryer

refrigerators

dishwashers

Why didn't we just put it out on the curb for the trashmen to pick up you ask? Well, lots of reasons. First, trash day in Southwest Philly was on a Friday and if we did the cleanout on a Tuesday and put the trash on the curb, Philadelphia's finest street inspectors would write you a "nuisance fine" of about $50 bucks for every day that it sat out there. Second, if we did put the trash out on Friday, the trashmen wouldn't pick up anything over 40 pounds, which left the metal still sitting on the damn curb. As far as the trash went, if you had more than six bags of trash out there, they'd want a kickback to take all of the bags. You know, roll a couple of $20 bills up in your palm and shake their hand so that they could take the money. What a scam! It was just easier to take it all to the dump and be done with it.

Finally, one day we caught what we thought was a break. We were carrying a stove out of one of our properties when a guy comes pulling up in an old, and I mean old, beat up truck. "Hey, you want that stove?" I say, "No, I'm throwing it out. Do you want it?" His eyes lit up like it was Christmas. "Sure, I'll take it." Then me, like a dummy says, "We have a bunch of metal in there if you want it." Well him and his partner couldn't get their asses out of that truck fast enough. He got every stitch of metal out of the house, shook my hand and gave me his card. He said, "Mr. if you get anymore metal, just call me and I'll come and get it!" As he got back into the truck and drove away, I didn't know who was happier, him or me? He was getting raggedy, rusted scrap metal and I no longer had to carry it out of my property, load it onto my truck, or best of all, pay to get rid of it! I now had it made in the shade.

stove break *Ernie's Truck*

Look, I'm not an idiot and I knew he was making a buck off the scrap, but I thought perhaps it was enough to get a tank of gas and maybe a bottle of wine if there was enough left over. Everyone of the guys who came around looking for scrap, looked, sounded, and acted the same way, right down to the same banged up trucks that they drove. I'm not trying to paint with a broad brush here but most of these guys wore horrible clothes, didn't have all of their teeth, drove worse trucks, and didn't seem like they had a college education (I can say that because I didn't make it there either, LOL.) Anyway, I just figured that they were making peanuts and I've got bigger fish to fry in the real estate world.

So now, let's flash forward about a year to 1998. My partner Nick and I are really starting to tear it up with these properties. By now, we've got about 35 of them under our belt and we're on our way, the sky is the limit! We make an investment in a stake body dump truck to make it easier on ourselves when we get to the dump. Of course, I'm still calling the scrap guy to come and get the metal but now when I get to the dump with the trash, I'm simply hitting the button on the dump truck and dumping the trash off. Before, we were loading the cans with trash, humping the cans onto our trucks, and when we got to the dump, we had to hand dump each and every can. What a pain in the ass it was! It was also very time consuming.

Best $5,500 I ever Spent!

It even Dumps!

Well one day we are cleaning out a property that we just purchased, and I call the scrap guy to come get the metal. He tells me that his partner got locked up and he asks me if my guys can bring the metal out to the curb and help him put it on his truck when he gets there.

He's a 60- year old guy, he's always done right by me, he was in a bind, so I agreed. He tells me he'd be there in about an hour. At the time, I was paying two, twenty-year old kids, a hundred bucks a day to help with the cleanouts. "Help" was an understatement! They'd bring everything out of the house and throw it on the stake body while Nick and I made our list of what needed to be done to the property, then me and Nick would take the trash to the dump and eat lunch. You've got to know how to work smart, ha!

So anyway, I tell the kids to start bringing all the metal out of the house first and put it on the curb for Ernie, which was the scrap guy's name. They bring out two refrigerators, a stove, dishwasher, 4 air conditioners, bed frames, and a bunch of other junk that was metal. As we're sitting out front of the house, a truck pulls up and the guy asks me if he can take the metal? I tell him no, it's spoken for. Ten minutes later another truck pulls up and then another truck. Two guys started arguing about who was there first and I tell them both, neither of you are getting it, somebody's already on their way here to get it. As they drove off, a lightbulb went off in my head that read, "Hey jerk-off, if all of these guys are fighting over this metal, don't you think it may be worth more than a tank of gas and a bottle of wine?"

So, with that, Here I am sitting there with a ton of metal, an empty truck that dumps very easily, and two strong, young guys that can throw the metal on my truck in ten minutes. Here is the best part, there are two scrap yards in Southwest Philly that are less then three minutes away from anyone of my properties. That is precisely the minute that I got into the scrap business! I told the two kids to take the gates off **my** truck and throw all the metal on. They, as well as Nick, looked at me like I had two heads. One of them said, "What about Ernie?" "Fuck Ernie, put it on there!" So much for doing right by me huh, LOL.

I got to the scrap yard, pulled on the scale and then I dumped the metal where they told me to. I weighed back in with an empty truck, they handed me a slip and told me to go inside and get my money. When they handed me the money, I'd like to shit, how about $237 bucks! Do any of you old timers remember the cartoon where Daffy Duck's head morphs into a jackass after he gives Bugs Bunny a million bucks? Well that is exactly how I looked.

For a solid year or so I'd been giving this money away and I felt like a fool. I don't care how much you make or how much you're worth, if you're giving it away, you're a fool! So goes the saying, "a fool and his money will soon part." Now, instead of reaching into my pocket and shelling out $200 bucks for the labor I had to pay the kids for cleaning out the house, I simply took it out of the scrap metal money and I even had enough money left over to buy us all lunch, what a deal! The hardest part was telling poor Ernie I wasn't going to be needing him anymore but oh well, he got over it and there is plenty, and I mean plenty, more scrap metal to go around!

That was just the start of my fever for scrap metal. My main gig is, was, and always will be real estate but I will no longer walk by, disrespect, throw away, or give away scrap metal. I now get it! That metal was not in my way, is wasn't trash, and it certainly wasn't slowing down my real estate project. In fact, I had to get rid of the metal anyhow, so it wasn't like I was stepping over dollars to pick up nickels. For now on, I'm going to be picking up the dollars and the nickels!

Since that eye opening day, I stated acquiring many smart and different ways to collect scrap metal. You may be asking, "What do you mean by a smart way to acquire scrap metal?" The answer to that is by not breaking your balls to get it! Most of the time, if you do it smart, you don't look for scrap, it finds you. Now that you know how I got started, I'm going to share with you some of my adventures over the past 20 years on how I go about making extra money in my spare time picking up that metal!

CHAPTER 4

THE EARLY BIRD CATCHES THE WORM

From the day that I caught *scrap metal fever*, my eyes began to open up wider and wider towards scrapping every day. I was making great money by now on my Section 8 Rentals, but I must have a bolt loose upstairs somewhere that constantly still makes me think about metal. One thing that I did notice was the day all the scrappers were usually cruising around the neighborhood and looking for scrap was Friday, which was trash day in Southwest Philly. I guess they drove around looking for something metal that the homeowners threw away. At about 9 o'clock in the morning, you'd see them driving down the street real slow, eyeballing up everyone's trash. I was busy working on my properties, so I wasn't a sidewalk seeker but don't get me wrong, if I was driving down the road and I saw something metal like a shelf or a dryer in someone's trash, I'd jump out of my truck and grab it.

Sidewalk Seeker's Dream

I'm and early riser and I'm usually saying goodnight to the owls when I head over to get my Wawa coffee at 5 o'clock in the morning. My workers don't start until 8 o'clock in the morning so I would usually shoot up to my shop at 5, do some paperwork, and get the materials set up for the day. Basically, I'm just trying to kill three hours until everyone arrives. Well one Friday morning I get a brainstorm. I said to myself, if these guys are searching the sidewalks at 9 o'clock, I'll beat them to the punch and get out there early.

I took a ride up a couple of streets and I hit the scrap jackpot! I was finding everything. Stoves, refrigerators, shelving, etc. I filled the stake body by myself in one hour, took the load to the scrapyard, and stuck $125 bucks in my pocket before 8 o'clock. Even know the trashmen wouldn't take the heavier appliances, I assume people still stick them out on the curb because they know that the scrappers will pick them up on trash day.

Now to be honest with you, I had to pass on a lot of the bigger, heavier objects like the refrigerators and washers. The dryers and some of the lighter stoves I could get up on the truck but the refrigerators, I think I left my balls next to them and never did they make it onto the back of the truck. I did however get the truck filled with a lot of the lighter metal like shelving, air conditioners, bikes, chairs and whatever else that was metal and light. Although it was lighter than the appliances, the lighter metal took up way more room in the back of the truck because it wasn't solid weight and it was awkward. I couldn't stack it as neatly as I could the appliances so then I got another idea.

What I did was ask one of the kids who helped me with the cleanouts if he wanted to work a couple hours on Friday mornings with me and I'd give him an extra $50 bucks. He agreed and we were off to the races! Now I was able to get those heavy refrigerators and appliances on the truck. These things took up less room and weighed a whole lot more which increased the profit. A truck load of appliances with light scrap mixed in was bringing me about $225. After paying my worker his $50, I was left with $175 which was $50 more than what I made by myself. Here's the best part, on some Fridays, we were able to get two full loads to the dump before 8 o'clock! I also invested in an awesome hand truck, (which I'll talk about later), that made it so simple that two anorexic guys could move a refrigerator. I was doing anywhere from $225 to $450 every Friday morning in three hours.

How can you beat that! I upped my worker's pay to $75 bucks a day to keep him interested, but now, I wanted more!

Common sense told me that the trashmen were full time and that they must have been working in some other part of the city Monday through Thursday. Now what that would mean is that people are throwing metal out in a different section of the city on these days and I wanted to get in on that as well. Where did they go? I had no idea, but I was going to find out! What I started doing was simple, I started searching for trash. Since I was up early, I'd drive around to different areas of the city to see if I could find out what day their trash day was. It didn't take me long and I was pleasantly surprised that on Thursday, trash day was at the lower end of Southwest Philly that I didn't invest in, but this area was only ten minutes from my shop, and Wednesday was trash day in a part of the city known as Grays Ferry which is only 15 minutes from my shop.

My worker and I started hitting these two sections of the city also. We could only get one load to the scrapyard instead of two because of the distance, which was fine with me. So for three mornings worth of work totaling about 9 hours, my weekly haul was around $850. After breaking my worker off $225 for his three days, I'd still walk with $625 a week, which I was thrilled with. A lot of people don't make that kind of paper in a week let alone nine hours. If you time's that by four, I was bringing in $2,500 a month on my morning runs, not to shabby!

Look, I have no incentive to blow smoke up your ass and the furthest thing in life I am is a bullshitter, I tell it like it is, not what you want to hear. There's money literally laying on the streets out there and all that you have too do is just get up earlier than the other guys and get it. Find out what day is trash day in your neck of the woods and get moving! If you snooze you lose. I'm telling you, the trick to getting scrap metal in this fashion is to get up early and get out the door. Most people who are going to throw away a heavy appliance will put it on the sidewalk the night before trash day, so it will be there early in the morning for you to grab and cash in.

If you're not an early riser, I already know what you're thinking. "I'll just stay up late and go grab it at 2 o'clock in the morning," right? Well don't, I already tried it and it's a total hassle. Number one, you've got bums that are still awake and want to ask you for change or worse yet, rob you. Number two, you've got night owl homeowners that are still awake and want to yell at you for making noise, especially in the summer time when everyone has their windows open. And number three, you have a heavy police presence at 2 o'clock in the morning. We got pulled over twice in one week for blocking the street and making noise.

5 o'clock is the perfect time to go get it! By 5 in the morning, the drunken bums have passed out, the night owl homeowners have gone to bed, and the police patrols have slowed down. It's a glorious time and there's nothing but rows and rows of beautiful metal sitting on the sidewalk, waiting for you to scoop up and cash in. Oh, and one more thing. If you're worried about what time the scrapyard opens, most open at 7 o'clock!

CHAPTER 5

MORE HOMES, MORE METAL!

All of my Section 8 homes are in the city of Philadelphia and so is my shop. Although this is where I conduct my business, this is not where I live. I live in the suburbs of Philadelphia, in a single home, not a rowhome. Here is why I am telling you this information. Just like real estate, the saying "location, location, location," is just as important when you are trying to hunt down scrap metal. Let me explain. One day my worker called out sick the night before. Since he wasn't going to make it in, I figured I'd take a shot at hunting down some scrap in my own neighborhood. Surely people had to throw something that was metal out in my neck of the woods too, so I was on my merry way out of the door at 5 a.m. to make some money.

Well, I probably burned off a half a tank of gas and I was only able to fill about a quarter of the truck. What a waste of time! It's not that people don't throw metal away in my neighborhood, they do, it's just that you have to drive around a hell of a lot longer to find it. I can drive down one small street in Philly, and it will have anywhere from 80 to

100 homes on the block. That's 100 homes that are potentially throwing away something that is metal. When the homes are spread out like they are in the Burbs, I might have to drive down twelve blocks before I pass by 80 homes, which is not only time consuming, but it puts a hell of a dent in your gas tank!

Make sure that when you scout out a neighborhood that you want to give a shot at potentially adding to your route, that the houses are somewhat close together. I'm not saying that they have to be rowhomes like in Philadelphia, but you want them pretty close together. The more affluent the neighborhood that you enter, the farther apart the homes are going to be, the less scrap you will find, the more gas you will burn, and the less profit you will see!

Philly averages about 80 homes per block

METAL MONEY

An affluent neighborhood will eat into your profit

CHAPTER 6

I CAUGHT A BRAKE, I MEANT BREAK

Be sure to Target Muffler and Brake Shops!

Believe me, I never considered growing my scrap business, it just happened by accident. Well, accident and my love for money and scrap metal, I guess. I was happy with the $2,500 bucks a month that I was making while killing off my mornings and while everyone else was sleeping. I was also very happy with my real estate investments as Nick and I continued to grow and grow into numbers that we both never fathomed were possible. I wasn't really looking to add onto my scrap metal route, when one day, it just happened. I was driving the stake body back to my shop and I hear the brakes start squealing. I call my brother Billy's buddy Dom who owns a brake and muffler shop and he tells me to bring the truck in.

When I get there, he tells me that the truck needed new brakes and rotors. I say okay, throw them on. He tells me it'll be about an hour, so I start shooting the shit with him as he does the job. When he gets all the rotors off, he yells over to his worker to get rid of them. The kid comes over, puts the brakes and rotors in a crate, takes them out the back door, and I think nothing of it. Anyway, about five minutes later my cell phone rings and it's too loud in the shop to hear, so I go out the back door to take the call. Well I look up at a ton of rotors in one pile and a mountain of mufflers in another pile. "Holy shit!" I said to myself.

Mount Muffler

Rising Rotors

I go back inside and I said, "Yo Dom, what the fuck is that out there, Mount Muffler?" He laughed and said, "Yeah, I got a guy that's suppose to come around every other week and get rid of the shit but he's a jerkoff, he only shows up every other month if I'm lucky. I pay him a hundred bucks to get rid of that shit, but I never see him." I said, "Are you kidding me? I'll get rid of it for ya for free!" He says, "You want it Mike, you got it, take it. I also own another one of these franchises in Northeast Philly with a ton of this crap sitting out back. If you want to go up there, you can have that scrap too."

I couldn't call my worker fast enough to get down to the brake shop. The minute my brakes were done, we loaded every single muffler and rotor that was in those piles and took them to the scrapyard. My brake job was $200 bucks which was a drop in the bucket compared to the cash we made off the scrap. After we took the brakes and rotors from the Northeast Philly store, we had a total of $1,100 bucks. I broke my worker off $300 and I was left with $800 bucks for six hours worth of work. Not bad work if you can get it!

That was a real heavy load, probably a couple of month's worth of scrap. Dom usually calls me every other week when he sees his piles getting a little high, and this location is good for about $600 bucks a month. Instead of calling me to tell me the pile is getting high, he might as well tell me to come pick up $300 bucks that's sitting on the ground out back because that is exactly what it equates to, but hey, I'm not complaining. Now let me tell you how you can do it!

CHAPTER 7

GETTING THE WORD OUT

I told you that after you are in this business for a while, you won't have to find scrap, scrap will find you! But first, you have to get some sort of word out and get your foot in the door and then your phone will start ringing. In the next couple of chapters, I'll tell you where and how to spread the word. But first you'll need three things. A company name and a "catchy" business name won't hurt, a business card, and a website. That's it and you're done! Most other businesses, you need a million things to get started. A scrap business only requires a couple of things to help you get the phone ringing.

Business Cards are Cheap and a Must

First, let's talk about your business name. Don't come up with something dreary or boring like "Mikes Recyclables". Why? Because people won't remember you. It's the slick, catchy names that people will remember and it will stick in their crawl. So, if they have say a washer and a dryer that they want to get rid of, they'll say, what was that guy's name again? Oh yeah, it was "Monster Metals" and they'll Google you on their phone and tell you to come and pick it up. "Mike's Recyclables" they'll forget you as fast as you can say I.

I even noticed it myself when I was at the scrapyard and I looked at the name on somebody's truck. I either forgot it a second later after I looked at it or it got stuck inside my warped brain. "Monster Metals" I thought was pretty clever and it's still floating around upstairs as well as some other's such as, "Scrap Attackers," "Leave the Cannoli, Take the Metal Recycling," "Can't Hack it, Scrap it". . . names like that, I'll never forget, and they'll be tangled up in my mind forever.

Now to the business card. Anyone can go online these days, grab a template, and make a business card. Just be sure that your name and number boldly stand out. Nobody wants to search through pictures of aluminum cans and copper pipes on your card to find the most important thing, which should be your phone number. The less busy your card is, the quicker the person will find your number.

Now to your webpage. First of all, don't get to carried away with your webpage and spend a ton of money. The only reason that you'll need a webpage is so that if someone throws away your card but remembers your name, your website will come up in a Google search. You might even get lucky if you live in a town, let's say Sharon Hill, and someone Google's "scrap metal collector near Sharon Hill." It's better to have a website than not have one at all but you really don't need one. If you do decide to have one created, keep it cheap, nothing fancy. Remember, you're collecting scrap, not designing kitchens. Again, the less busy the better. Boldly list your name, phone number, and tell them that you'll come and remove the metal from their home or business for **free**! If you want to tell people that you are going to charge them a service fee to pick up their metal, I promise you, your phone won't ring. There are to many guys out here doing it for free and if you want to compete, keep it free or find a new side hustle.

Anyway, when you get these three things in place, and it shouldn't take long, you're ready to hit the concrete and begin making more money! Now let me tell you a couple of great places to get started. Let's start with Muffler and Brake shops as well as automotive garages and autobody shops. That's right, since my brother's buddy hooked me up with his two stores, I started knocking on other Brake and Muffler shops doors like Midas, Bargain Brakes and Mufflers, Meineke Mufflers, etc. You would think that since they are such a big company that somebody would come around and grab their scrap for them. Fortunately, that's simply not the case. Believe it or not, most of these stores are franchised and owned by everyday guy's trying to make it in the business world.

They were just like me at one time, to busy or consumed by their own business that they didn't have time for the small stuff like taking a load of metal to the scrapyard. I'd knock on their door, introduce myself, shake their hand, and hand them my card. Some of them would tell me to hit the road but mostly everyone of them would take my card and tell me if they had anything, they'd give me a call. Then, a weird thing started happening about a week later. My phone started to ring!

I wasn't lighting the world on fire by any means, but I'd say my success rate was about 10%, not bad. I have the gift of gab, a great sense of humor, and I'm not afraid to talk to anyone so I'm sure that increases my percentages a little bit. So anyway, I thought that if 10% of the brake and muffler shops were willing to play ball, maybe I could get my foot in the door at some autobody shops.

Autobody Shops always have some Scrap laying around

Once again, I started beating the sidewalks and knocking on some doors. Again, I ran into some ignorant pricks who run you out of their shop faster than you can turn the knob to get in, but I also had a lot of guys that took my card and told me that they'd give me a call. Here is another thing that I'd like to add. Don't be afraid to hear someone out either. If they try to swing a 50/50 split deal on the metal with you and you can still make some cash, go for it! Some cash is better than no cash. I'm going to say that my success rate stuck at about 10% and my phone continued to ring as I added some healthy stops to my scrap route. Now here's the best part and the part that I told you about, how scrap finds you! After you beat on someone's door and you get your foot into that door, scrap will start to find you. How? By word of mouth.

After the initial time of finding your donor, they now start calling you and ringing the dinner bell. All you have to do now is go pick up their metal and cash it in at the scrapyard. How easy can it get? Wait, it gets even easier! Business finds business and once you get your foot in the door, you never know what can happen. Once I started making friends and getting to know some of the automotive shop owners who were giving me their metal, other doors started opening for me. They'd tell one or two of their friends that were also in the business that I pick up their scrap for free, I'm reliable, and I'm a decent guy, and then my phone really started to blow up!

Word of mouth is key in this game and if you're reliable, word will spread like wildfire, that I guarantee. By now, I added six more locations and I was getting at least four calls a week from my automotive stops which typically brought in about $50 bucks per stop, equaling $200 per week and $800 bucks per month. Back out my helpers pay and I'm at about $600 bucks per month. Now let's do some math. That's $600 a month, plus the $600 per month I was making off Dom's Muffler shop, plus the $2,500 per month from my Southwest Philly morning runs which comes to a total of $3,700 bucks a month that I was pulling in for about 18 to 20 hours worth of work a week!

By now, I really had the metal flu and I wanted to get every last screw that was laying out on the street, waiting for me to cash in at the yard. I started thinking outside the box and coming up with some more clever ways to land that scrap!

CHAPTER 8

THINKING OUTSIDE THE METAL BOX

By now, you may be scratching your head and thinking, "What's wrong with this guy? He owns over 300 homes and it sounds like he likes scrap metal money more than real estate money?" You would be wrong, I love all money equally. I do love the fact that the scrap money is free! However, I will tell you this, I have never put scrapping before real estate. I know what puts the most butter on my bread, so let's say I had to pick a large order up at Home Depot early on a Thursday morning so my carpenter would have materials to work with, I'd blow off scraping that morning.

Here is the best part of real estate and why people choose to own it. It gives you a ton of free time! Once I have a house up and rented, I do one of two things. I either look for another home to purchase or I look for more places to find scrap metal, I'm always on the prowl! Sure, I have to do my daily tasks, like go down the Section 8 office and sign a lease, or deal with my contractors, or deal with a pain in the ass tenant, but I've been doing it for so long now that I know how to jam it all into about a five hour day. My scrap metal adventures start at 5 a.m., which is 3 hours before my contractors show up for work and it's 4 hours before the Section 8 office even opens their doors. I'm usually done everything that I have to do by 1 o'clock in the afternoon, but rather than go home and watch T.V. or mope around the shop, I go out and pick up metal or brainstorm another way to find it!

Section 8 opens their doors four hours after I start my scrap runs.

Okay, I thought to myself, the automotive field doesn't mind me picking up their metal so who can I branch out to next? I started thinking of other businesses that are metal based and I came up with a good amount of them. I wrote them down on a sheet of paper and then I started looking them up on the internet and writing down their addresses so I could go pay them a visit. I don't like cold calling places because you get nowhere. . .fast. I know because I tried this angle also. I'd barely get the words, "I'm looking for the owner of the company" out of my mouth before they'd tell me to kiss their ass and hang up on me. I can't imagine what they'd say if they'd actually let me get to the point where I told them that I want them to give me their metal, LOL. I'm sure they'd of thrown a couple of F bombs at me. Oh well, I'm use to it from my tenants. My phone success rate was a big fat 0% so don't even waste your time.

Anyway, I started looking up machine shops, wrought iron railing shops, spiral staircase shops, sheet metal fabricators, heating and duct manufactures, etc. Anyone that worked with metal and might have had some scrap lying around, I jumped in my truck and visited. Again, I started knocking on doors, being told to get lost more than once, but most importantly, putting my phone number into potential customers hands.

When I pulled up to this one certain machine shop, I didn't even have a chance to scratch my ass when this giant of a man came barreling out of the door carrying a large metal can, and he was nasty too boy! "What the fuck do you want?," he says. He was an older guy of about 65 years old. He stood at least 6 foot 6 and his hands looked like he was wearing two catcher's mitts. As he was dumping out the drum, I tell him I just wanted to know if he had any scrap metal laying around and I'd be willing to take it away for free. "Free" he snapped, "Fuck Free, are you willing to work for it?"

Ray's Machine Shop

I'll save you all the other curse words that he hurled at me and tell you what it led to. What it led to was me coming to his machine shop every Friday night to help him clean out his machines. Every Friday night from 4 p.m. until 6 p.m., I'd help him pull heavy, soaking wet with oil, brass flakes from all his machines. He had some sort of contract with a bolt company where he made all their nuts and bolts. We'd fill one and sometimes two of these pretty good sized cans and he'd let me keep what they were worth in scrap. That's where the, "are you willing to work for it" part came into play.

METAL MONEY

*These are the size of the brass flakes that
we would remove from Ray's machines.*

The minute we'd get done, I'd run a drum or two down to the scrapyard (most don't close until 7 o'clock). The first time that I cashed them in, I couldn't believe it! I was now cashing in brass which was worth way more than scrap metal but still, my eyes popped out of my head when the cashier told me it was worth $400 bucks.

That's $400 bucks for two hours worth of work! The next week when I went back to the shop to see Ray, which is his name, I said, "Ray, they gave me $400 bucks for that shit, let me at least split it with ya." He says, "No way Mike, I know what it's worth, it's yours, keep it. I offered everyone of the lazy bums that work for me to help me on Friday nights, but everyone of them runs out of here like their ass is on fire to get to the bar so I'm glad you knocked on my door."

Turns out Ray wasn't as nasty as I thought he was. He's a stubborn old guy, yells a lot, and wants things done his way but hey, for $200 bucks an hour I'll do it anyway that he wants me to do it!

I also got a call back from the spiral staircase company who give me a pretty big load every month and I did get another call from a heating company that manufactures duct work. I picked up their scrap twice and then, if you can believe it, I had to dump them. The sheet metal was light and if you didn't squash it down properly in the truck, it took up a ton of room. Squashing it was time consuming and my feet ended up hurting from stomping on it. The big kicker was I only made thirty bucks on each run. You've got to know when to fish or cut bait and, in this scenario, I cut bait.

So as you can see, all along the way here I keep adding a customer or two which keeps my phone ringing and adds to my monthly scrap salary. Just by adding Ray's machine shop and the spiral staircase accounts, it added on another $2,000 bucks a month. If you're doing the math at home and add this to my $3,700 a month that I was already bringing in, that's a whopping monthly total of $5,700 bucks a month, and it keeps getting better!

These are just a couple of companies that I thought of that use metal in their business. If you can think of more, which I'm sure that you can, write them down, look up their address, and go pay them a visit. You'll get a fair amount of assholes who are rude and tell you to get out but never, ever let that deter you. You only have to be right once, and it can lead to bigger and better things for you. I used to laugh to myself when some of the businesses would pin the "managers tag" on a guy and he'd go out of his way to be a dick to me, as if he were better than me because he was the head honcho of "Bob's Muffler's". He'd act like I was a dirt bag who was asking him for his first born when all that I was asking him for was scrap metal. I'd walk out of there thinking asshole, if you only knew what kind of money that I'm making from scrapping part time you'd pass out. If I sprung on him how many homes I own and what kind of paper I'm worth from my full time gig he'd probably drop dead.

Anyway, my point is to keep being creative and think of any business that you can target and take a shot at them, you've got nothing to lose and everything to gain. A lot of people who own businesses aren't lazy, they just don't have the time to sweat the small stuff like getting rid of scrap and they may be looking for a guy just like you to get rid of it for them. Once they become a customer and you treat them right, they become a customer for life!

CHAPTER 9

DUMPSTER DIVING

Well, I owe this tip to my worker. I'll stop calling him my worker at this point in the book because his name is Rob and he's become not only a great worker and a loyal friend, but he also has a pretty creative head on his shoulders when it comes to inventive ways of finding scrap metal.

One day we were driving down the road and he says to me, "Mike, pull into that industrial park and let's scout out the dumpsters." I really didn't want to but just to appease him I said, what the hell. Well as we pulled up to the dumpster area, we knew that we made a pretty good score! There were 14 steel desks, a bunch of old scaffolding, and a ton of steel shelving all piled up on the ground around the dumpsters. It took us two trips to get it all and I believe we picked up over $400 bucks on that score.

Steel Shelving *Heavy Steel Desks*

Since it was Rob's idea to drive through the industrial park, I split the money right down the middle with him, $200 apiece. I'm not greedy and I'll take $200 for two hours worth of work any day. Splitting the money with Rob was both a good thing and a bad thing for me. Let me explain the good part first.

After the 50/50 split, Rob asks me, "Mike, if I keep locating the metal, will you keep us on a 50/50 split with the metal that I lead us to? I answer, "Absolutely, you find it, we split it." It worked out great for about two years. We still did our morning thing where I'd pay him $75 bucks per morning to drive through Southwest Philly with me but whenever we'd take a run through on of the industrial parks he discovered, I'd split the money evenly with him.

To Rob's credit, he really started getting creative and locating more and more industrial parks to drive through. On his own time, he would drive through them to see if anything was being left out that was worth scrapping. If there are any industrial parks near you, make sure that you start checking their dumpsters. Almost every single time that we would drive through them, we'd hit a homerun!

Industrial Parks are Loaded with Scrap!

Most industrial parks are filled with factories and offices and they're constantly throwing away shelving, scaffolding, desks, chairs, metal cabinets, etc. I guarantee you that you'll make some cash on every run, so I tip my hat to Rob on this one.

Once a hustler gets a good taste of money, they get like a vampire gets when he taste's blood, they want more of it! The more money that we'd split, the more creative ideas Rob would come up with. One day he says to me, "Let's go out tonight and start checking the dumpsters of some of the muffler and autobody shops that never called you back. I said, "Sure, what the hell." Damn if this kid wasn't right again! He's like a bloodhound when it comes to sniffing out metal. Anyway, we pay a visit to a couple of the body shops and muffler shops and we end up almost filling the truck with what was thrown away in their dumpsters. I take it to the yard the next day and cash the ticket for $250 bucks, $125 apiece for a couple hours of dumpster diving!

Always check what's in a dumpster!

That's the next tip in this chapter. Just because you were turned down by someone from giving you their scrap, it doesn't mean that you can't take it out of their dumpsters at night if they throw it away. If there's metal in the dumpster, load it up and take it. Now I'm not telling you that if their dumpster is behind a closed or locked gate to walk right in and grab it, but if the dumpster is right out front of the place for anybody to route through, I'm gonna be the guy doing the rooting!

Some guys are such pricks that they'd rather throw the metal away than give it to you. They're too lazy to scrap it themselves but they don't want to see you make a buck either, how selfish and stupid! I'm glad that I'm not lazy, in fact, I'd rather be stupid than lazy. If you're stupid instead of lazy, at least you'll get up off your ass and go out and make a buck. Thank God I'm neither! Where was I now? Oh yeah, I was rambling on about lazy people choosing to throw away scrap metal instead of giving it away.

So the more money Rob starts making, I start to see a fire in his eyes. This kid has the scrap fever like I have the Section 8 real estate fever. He starts coming up with more and more ways to make money in this business and now that leads us into the bad part of the 50/50 split!

It's good for me, business wise, when he continues to find scrap, but now, I'm starting to get worried because I can see the handwriting on the wall. After splitting the money with him, he now sees what kind of money that I'm pulling in on these runs and I know that it's just a matter of time before the kid goes out and purchases the same type of truck as me and does it on his own. I know that it's coming and if I were him, I'd do the same damn thing! Let's get to another one of Rob's awesome tips before he rolls out the door on me.

CHAPTER 10

HOLIDAY SCRAP

Okay, I told you that I scrap in the city because there are way more homes, obviously more volume equals more metal. However, there is one week when I keep my scrap hunt confined to the suburbs. That week would be the week after Memorial Day and I also owe this tip to Rob.

As winter turned to spring one year, Rob says to me, "Hey Mike, ya know what I've been noticing on my way into work? I'm starting to see a lot of gas grills, lawnmowers and beach chairs in people's trash." Now Rob also commutes from the suburbs into the city every morning so if he says he's seeing grills, he's seeing grills. I said, "Yeah Rob, but I'm not going to ride through the 'burbs for a grill or two when I know that we can fill the truck up on any given day in the city." He says, "Mike, I'm telling you, we will get a ton of grills, I'm seeing them all over the place!" He says, "I used to work at Sears and after people's grills sit all winter, a lot of them won't fire up. People usually throw away their old grill and go out and get a new one in the spring." Well, usually the first barbeque of the year for everyone is on Memorial so let me tell you what happened.

This kid has been right on so many other occasions, and by now, I know that he has a knack for the scrap metal field. Listen, I sit up and think about how to make more money with real estate investments and he sits up and thinks of where to find scrap, everyone has their talents. The reason that he wanted to drive through the Burbs, as opposed to Southwest Philly, the entire week after Memorial Day is because more people have pools and yards in the Burbs. Obviously, more people with yards and pools are going to be barbequing. He hit the nail on the head again!

We drove around every morning the Tuesday after Memorial Day, until Friday and we loaded up so many grills that I lost count. Of course, I'd much rather fill the truck with grills instead of scrap metal because you make more cash! The lid and the bottoms of most grills are cast aluminum which is worth six times more than plain scrap. The top lid rips right off and we'd bring a cordless grinder with us to grind off a couple of the bolts so we could remove the cast aluminum bottom. The entire process takes two minutes but it's well worth it! At this moment, scrap is worth 7 cents a pound and cast aluminum is worth 45 cents a pound, so you do the math and tell me if it's worth it? We were also able to load up a bunch of aluminum lawn chairs and lawn mowers. I guess the plastic on the lawn chairs rot out from sitting and the lawnmowers have reached the end of their life span.

Memorial Day Grill Hunt!

If the week after Memorial Day is a great time to find grills, the week after Thanksgiving is an awesome time to go out hunting for stoves. A lot of people simply don't cook all year long but when Thanksgiving rolls around, everyone's a chef! When they turn their oven on and it's shot and can't be fixed, it ends up on the sidewalk for me to grab. I'd always notice a spike in stoves the week after Thanksgiving. Nothing like the spike in grills after Memorial Day, but a spike non the less.

Now, Let's talk about Christmas. Forget it! The week before Christmas, you have every scrapper and their brother out at all hours of the night trying to hustle a buck, and guess what? There's way less scrap this time of year. Why? Because people aren't cleaning out their basements or doing projects the week before Christmas, they try to get projects done before the holidays so that they can enjoy them. They're either partying, visiting, or having family and friends over so you're far less likely to find a lot of scrap metal this week.

The week following Christmas isn't much better. You won't find hardly any metal but there's going to be a ton of trash on the sidewalks, and I mean a ton! It'll be a clutter fuck, trust me. People are eating, drinking, and unwrapping presents. This leads to a ton of empty gift boxes and trash bag after trash bag of smelly spoiled food and beer bottles. Take these two weeks, the week before and after Christmas, off and relax. The scrap metal, without all the garbage will return a week or so after the holidays and you can go back to making the money!

Handsome tree and a handsome Guy!

CHAPTER 11

SCHOOL'S OUT!

Right after Rob and I get done cleaning up on disposed grills after Memorial Day, we can't wait for the next big payday, which is summer vacation! Here's how we stumbled upon this great tip.

I live down the street from a high school. It was the 2nd week of June and school had just let out for the summer. As I drove by the school, I looked over at the dumpster area. It was filled with so much metal that they were stacking it in car parking spots! Desks, lockers, chairs, shelving, etc. I got rob on the horn and that night we cleared it out and lined our pockets. I thought it was just going to be a one- time thing but fortunately, I was wrong!

High School, better known as "Metal High"

The next day, more metal and the day after was the same. So now, seeing that two great minds think alike, we took a shot and visited some more school's dumpster areas. Bingo! They all had something in them which was worth our while. This went on for about three weeks before it started to slow down.

So one day, I'm doing my scouting rounds when I see a custodian who worked for the school. He was wheeling a teacher's desk out on a hand truck. I ask him if he's tossing it and he says, "Yes, and there's four more in there that I'm getting rid of."

I tell him I'll be back in 20 minutes with my helper and stake body and I ask him, "Do you guy's throw this kind of stuff out all year?"

He answers, "No, when school lets out, we get rid of all of the broken desks and lockers that can't be fixed. It usually takes us about a month to replace them."

He was spot on, by July 4th it dried up and we were luck if we found a copper BB in their trash. However, we do clean up every year for the first month that school lets out. Now, we are smart enough to make a list of the schools in the area and cruise by them to see what's going on. Like I said, there is always something there that will make your trip worth while. I really don't have any colleges near me that I could put on the list, but rest assured, if there was a college near me, it'd be on the list and I'd hit them too!

CHAPTER 12

LEARN THE TRASH ROUTE

I'm going to start this chapter out by saying thank God my scrap partner was a loyal friend! Just like I anticipated, it happened. Rob and I were scrapping one day and he says to me, "Mike, I'm thinking about buying a truck and going out on my own. Are you going to be pissed at me?" I laughed and said, "Rob, I don't know why you didn't do it sooner."

Look, I don't want to sound like a big shot here, but scrap metal is fun money to me. It's something that I started doing to occupy myself for 3 hours because I get up before the crack of dawn. Now don't get me wrong, by the time that Rob broke the news to me that he was pulling out, I was pulling down an extra six to seven thousand a month, which is good, especially if you like playing craps at the casino and betting on football like me, a couple of other passions of mine, LOL, but in all honesty, I really didn't want to see it go away.

I figured that I could still scrap by myself, but I surely would be making less, and it wouldn't be as fun. Rob's a strong guy and can damn near throw the appliances onto the back of the truck by himself, without the hand truck! I knew that I'd be picking up way less scrap without him on my morning runs, not to mention the other scrap he sniffs out. Well it was at that time, while I was running those scenarios through my head, that Rob said this to me. "Mike, I'm still going to do all of our morning runs together with you and hit our normal stops. Just after you start your real estate gig at 8 o'clock, I'm going to jump into my truck and stay out here scrapping."

Man, what a relief it was to hear that! But also, I guess that he played it smart. By now, he was making a grand or better a week with me, and if he could go out on his own and hustle another grand, more power to him. Plus, I always let him use my Porsche whenever he wants to impress one of his dates, so I guess he didn't want to lose that privilege (shameless plug)!

Fake it Until You Make it, LOL!

So here is what Rob did. Once it hit 8 o'clock in the morning and I put my Section 8 landlord hat on, I was done thinking about scrap metal for a while. However, Rob was jumping into his new truck to see what he could find out there. His main problem he told me was not so much running into the late starting, lazy scrappers, but running into traffic and trashmen.

Rob's new Truck

By 8 o'clock, the trashmen were getting their day started and they were beating him to the punch! Some streets that he would drive up, the trashmen already visited and collected everything on the street. I told you that the trashmen wouldn't take heavy appliances but light metal, which we made a good buck on, would be thrown into the back of the garbage truck. That was one of the negatives and here is another. Sometimes, he'd turn up a street and the trash truck would already be on it collecting trash. Now when a car pulls in behind you on the smaller streets, you're trapped and there is nowhere to go. You sit there and watch helplessly as the trashmen throw metal object after metal object onto their truck! You're literally sitting there not only losing money, but watching it get thrown away right in front of your face. Just like in any other business, time is money and it's no different in the scrap business. If you're sitting behind a trash truck, you're not finding scrap, you're burning gas, and another scrapper is beating you to the punch!

Stuck behind a Trash Truck

Rob got totally fed up with getting caught in traffic, getting stuck behind trash trucks, and driving down streets that had already been picked up, so here's what he did. Instead of taking his stake body out one morning, he took his car and notebook with him. He followed the trashmen from their starting point at 7 a.m., which was at their headquarters, up until 12 o'clock in the afternoon. He logged every move that they made, what time they went down a street and what street that they hit next, what time they went to the dump, etc. He knew that they were on a schedule and he wanted to stay in front of them rather than behind them.

For now on, after he jumped out of my truck at 8 o'clock, he was going to be prepared! He knew where the trashmen *were not* and those were the streets that he'd start hitting because the trashmen did not get to them until later. The trashmen have a route and a schedule that they keep, and they stick to it and don't change it. They're like the Brinks truck drivers. If you ever want to knock them off, you can set your watch to these guys and it's the same with the trashmen. I'd suggest that you stick to scrapping metal though, an armored car heist will get you about 20 years.

Anyway, if curb metal collecting is one of the routes that you are going to take in your quest to obtain money scrapping, then make sure that you stay one step ahead of the trashmen. You don't want them beating you to a shred of metal and eating into your profits!

CHAPTER 13

SCRAP METAL HOUSE CALLS

I'll tell you right now, I only tried it once and I'll never do it again! Here's the story. My sister's friend hears that I'm in the scrap metal business, so she rings my phone. "Mike, it's Tracy, I've got a couple of refrigerators in my basement and a bunch of metal in my garage if you want to swing by and grab it." It was a Saturday in the dead of winter, and I wasn't doing anything, so I said sure, what the hell, I'll help her out. Big mistake!

When I get there, her husband, who is the guy who is going to be helping me, let's me in the door. As soon as I lay eyes on him, I knew that I was in for a fun day. He was about 125 pounds and looked like a jockey! Not only that but he also looked like his profession was an accountant because I imagine the only thing that this guy ever carried in his life were numbers. So, we get started.

First, after taking ten minutes to help me move the refrigerator six or seven feet over to the steps, I find out that the refrigerator won't fit up the steps. They had their basement finished at one point and framed out the wall going up the steps. When I asked him if he had any tools in the basement so we could get the door off, he looked at me like I had two heads. Thank God I carry tools in my truck, but I had to go back outside and get them, remove the door, and then carry the refrigerator up the steps with Skinny Vinny. As if that wasn't bad enough, he must have told me 55 times to "watch the walls."

Finally, by the time we get the thing up the steps, his wife starts telling me to watch the hardwood floors, she doesn't want them scratched and of course, "watch the walls." By the grace of God, we get the damn thing out of the house and into the back of my truck and I head back in for more abuse. I need this torture like I need another asshole.

I pull out my tape measure and I measure the second refrigerator and I tell him the same thing, it's not going to fit, the door also has to come off of this one. He twists his ugly little face up and says, "Are you sure?," as if he's going to be the guy doing the work. "No jerk-off, I don't know how to read a tape measure," is what I wanted to say but I bit my tongue and stayed calm. I said, "Of course I'm sure, do you want to measure it yourself?"

His next sentence was his last that I could put up with. I kid you not, he says, "Just be a little more careful with this one, you almost scratched the floors. You've got insurance though, right?"

First of all, how do you *almost* scratch a floor, and secondly, no, I don't have insurance for this bullshit! I immediately stopped taking the door off the refrigerator and threw my tools back in the bag without saying a word to him. I grabbed my hand truck and while I was pulling it up the steps, he has the balls to say, "You're taking this one too, right?" I told him to go fuck himself and when I got to the top of the steps, Tracy says, "What did you say to him?" I return with, "The same thing I'm telling you, go fuck yourself, you people are nuts!"

Neither one of them have talked to me or my sister again and I never stepped foot into another homeowner's house again to collect metal. It's just not that worth it to me. I don't need to be taking orders from homeowners, taking doors off refrigerators, getting my nerves shot about scratching walls or floors, and being asked to produce insurance papers!

If I'm breaking my balls in somebody's house for an hour trying to get a refrigerator out the door, I'd better get way more money then what the refrigerator is worth in scrap! Like I said, I got a bolt loose in my head when it comes to free money and I don't think things out sometimes. The money ain't too free if the homeowner is a pain in the ass and they think that they own you the minute that you step into their home, even if you're doing them the favor of dragging a 350- pound refrigerator up their steps!

Rob has also collected scrap from homeowners. He now and then runs an add on Craigslist, but he also will no longer dig appliances out of homeowner's basements. He's on the same page as me. It's to time consuming and you never know what you're getting yourself into! There is so much stuff laying on the streets that you don't have to go into someone's home and lug a refrigerator up 12 steps, so why bother? Go the easy route!

CHAPTER 14

TO SEPARATE OR NOT TO SEPARATE THAT IS THE QUESTION!

I've been scrapping metal for quite some time now and I'm pretty good at it, but not great. My strong points are I'm reliable, I know where to find scrap, and I have a great personality with the gift of gab, to get my foot in the door of some of the business that need their scrap picked up. When I get to the scrapyard, I see and meet guys who are great at scrapping! There's a ton of jerk-offs down there but I also meet a good amount of guys who know the scrap business like it's the back of their hand, it's their profession.

These guys can look at a piece of metal and tell what type it is, what it came from, what it's worth today, and what time of year that it's value will be at its peak. They can look at my scrap load and tell me within 50 pounds of what it weighs. The reason that they can do this is that scrap is their livelihood, it's how they make a living. They're at it 12 hours a day, six days a week, and it's a good thing that the scrapyard is closed on Sunday, otherwise they'd be at it seven days a week!

Me, I'm not into it like that. I'm happy picking up 6 or 7 grand a month in my spare time. The reason that I'm telling you this is, I'd always feel guilty when I'd scrap, say an air conditioner, and some of these experts would be in the pile next to me and they'd say, "Yo Boss, you're leaving a lot of meat on the bone. You're only getting scrap weight for this. You should strip it down, you've got copper tubes in there, a steel canister and motor, and you can separate the wiring."

This is how I Scrap an Air Conditioner

Of course, I already know that copper and aluminum is worth more than scrap metal, but I just don't have the time or energy to get into it like that because then, it really becomes work to me! I do enough work starting at 8 o'clock when I have to put up with my tenants and contractors. The fulltime scrappers are the experts and I'm just trying to steer you in the right direction with this book. If you do have the time, do it right and separate the metal to receive the maximum profit. If you're scrapping a sink, snap the copper lines off it. If you're scrapping an air conditioner, rip it open and get everything that you can out of it. I watched a YouTube video entitled, "how to scrap an air conditioner" and my asshole clinched up on how much money I lose. This guy had the thing on the ground and separated into six different piles quicker than a hooker can undo a belt. Anyway, to make a long story short, for the same 3 bucks that I get for scrap metal from the air conditioner, this guy gets 22 bucks for separating it, not bad! I was already doing the correct thing with the gas grills but that's because it took two seconds to rip the cast aluminum tops off. Had it taken more than two seconds, the grills probably would have ended up in the scrap metal pile also, LOL.

This is how a Pro Scraps an Air Conditioner!

I watch some of these guys at the scrapyard get down and dirty and I'm amazed! Remember when you were a kid and watched a movie on how an American Indian would shoot a bear and nothing would go to waste? He'd eat the meat, he'd use the fur as a blanket or rug, the teeth and bones he'd use as tools, the paw he'd use as a back scratcher and the blood he'd use for his face as warpaint. Well, that's how these guys are with scrap. They'll strip everything down into four or five different piles. I'm afraid to stand still next to them to long in fear that they might strip me down to my boxers!

If you've got all day to do it like these guys, by all means, do it right and increase your profits and make every cent that you can. If you have a fulltime gig like me and you've got to get your ass to work, kick the metal off the back of the truck, be happy with what ever they give you, and be on your merry way. So what I guess that I'm trying to say is, there is no right or wrong answer to the question, "to separate or not to separate." It's what works best for you, your schedule, and how far that you want to take it. Either way, you're always going to make a buck!

CHAPTER 15

PICKING OFF OF THE PILE

I don't get it, I don't agree with it, and I'll never understand it, but if you want to make an easy $100 bucks in about 4 hours, jump right in the pile and do it! First of all, for you novice, let me explain what "picking off the pile" means. Let's say that I pull into the scrapyard with a load of scrap metal that I'm going to scrap for 6 cents per pound. A yard worker will point me into a clear area where I can dump my truck. As soon as that shit (the metal) hits the ground, I swear, these

Pile Picker

guys rise up from the ground like a zombie and start rummaging through my scrap!

Like I talked about in the previous chapter, let's say that I scrap an air conditioner that I'm getting 3 bucks for in scrap. Well these are the guys that will filet the damn thing into five different piles and take it to the different stations within the scrapyard and get 22 bucks. How the hell does this make sense and how the hell does the scrapyard make any money off it if they are giving me 3 bucks and him 22 bucks? That's 25 bucks that they are giving up for that air conditioner. If I scrap a sink, they'll pull anything that's copper off it and put it in their copper bucket that they carry around with them. They'll pull the copper off so fast that if you blink, you'll miss it! If I throw away a desk, they'll rip the brass handles off it and put them in their brass bucket. A screen door, once again, the brass handle gets yanked and thrown in the bucket. Old windows, the frames will be taken over to the aluminum cashier.

Scrap to me, Aluminum Jackpot to Pile Picker!

These aren't guys that work for the scrapyard either, they're just guys who show up at the yard, comb through piles of scrap all day that have already been dumped, and pull pieces of more valuable metal, such as copper, brass, and aluminum, off less valuable metal like steel and tin. It's the little pieces of metal that most people don't want to take the time out to remove (and I'm one of them), that these pile pickers feast off of!

These guys are in the pile all day, pulling little pieces of precious metals, and at the end of the day, it all adds up. Look, I talk to everyone, I'd talk to Charles Manson if he was alive and picking off the pile. I love to bullshit with these guys and ask them what kind of coin they're making a day doing this. I didn't talk to a single one who said that they were making less then $100 bucks a day!

First, you have to make sure that the scrapyard you're doing it at permits it, of course, or they'll throw you out of there. I've been to at least five different scrapyards in Philly and two in Delaware and I've never seen anyone tell these guys to get the hell out of the pile, so in some way the yard must be benefiting from this. Sometimes, they get so anxious trying to see what you have on the back of your truck that they get in the way when you're trying to dump it. I tell them, "Stay the hell out of the way until the scrap hits the ground, then it's all yours!"

The smarter guys walk around with battery operated tools and they clean up. I'll discuss this in the next chapter. They fill a couple of five-gallon buckets worth of copper and brass and they cash them in, all day! How can you go wrong? You don't have to go out looking for scrap, morons like me that don't separate will bring it right to you. If the scrap yard is going to permit it, have fun, make money, and knock yourself out!

Pile Pickers fill these Buckets all Day Long!

Here is the part that I don't get, and I'll never understand. Isn't it like double dipping? I mean, if they pay me 5 cents a pound for the metal and a guy breaks off a 2 pound brass bolt and cashes it in for 2 bucks, wouldn't the scrapyard be losing money because the paid both of us? I guess the answer to that question is no or they wouldn't be letting them do it. If anyone has the answer to this question, email it to me and I'll put it in my next book. There's that loose bolt of mine again, worrying about money that's not even mine. I'm sick I tell ya, sick!

METAL MONEY

CHAPTER 16

TOOLS NEEDED FOR PICKING OFF THE PILE

With these 3 tools, you can make a fortune, picking off the pile. But before we get started here, I'll let you know this. I see about 2 or 3 guys in that pile who know what they're doing, the rest of them that are in the pile are hand-jobs! If you're gonna be in that pile, tearing things apart for a living, and you don't have the right tools, stay the hell out of it!

I've seen it all down there. There's one guy that they call Thor, he's been down there for years and he walks around with a plastic trashcan and a gigantic sledge hammer. If he sees any precious metal still attached to the metal that you dumped, if he can't break it off with his bare hands, he'll clobber it to death with his sledge hammer until it falls off. Then he'll stick that piece in his bucket and move along to beating the shit out of something else for a half hour. He might beat on something for an hour just to free a piece of copper worth a buck, a real winner! However, he's in great shape and gets a good workout in every day.

Thor's only Tool!

Then there's a couple of other one's who actually do carry around a bucket of tools, from the 1950s! They probably found the tools in the pile and I believe that Fred Flintstone has a more modern set of tools then these guys. You'll see them with a 30 year-old hacksaw, taking 20 minutes to cut copper lines off a sink or trying to snap a bolt off a bracket with a ballpeen hammer and chisel. Who the hell still uses ballpeen hammers? It's nuts!

It's nuts, but these guys continue to make $100 bucks a day. Do you know why? Because they are successful by default! The reason that they are successful by default is because of jackasses like me that don't strip their metal. There is enough metal being dumped at their feet, that they are going to salvage a little piece of something off a lot of pieces of everything. They're tripping over it all day long! These little pieces add up to their buckets getting filled, which in turn, adds up to their pockets getting filled.

Now let's talk about the 2 or 3 guys in that pile who really earn some cash! These guys also come to the yard with a bucket of tools, but these guys come to win! They simply bring tools that get the job done fast. Sure, everyone has a hammer and other junk in their bucket but the three main ingredients these guys have is a cordless Sawzall, cordless screw gun, and a cordless grinder.

If you push something off your truck that has meat on the bone, these guys will flip it over and go to work! They'll cut into it with the Sawzall, open it up, strip out all the good stuff and put it in their bucket, leave the carcass, and move onto the next payday within two minutes. If the other guys are making $100 a day down there jerking-off, triple that amount for these guys! When I watch the experts work, it always reminds me of a day that I went out on a deep see fishing tour. We hit a school of bluefish and everyone on the boat caught about 20 fish. All I could think of, on the way in, was a lot of my meat was going to go to waste because it would take a long time for me to clean 20 fish and I really didn't want to do it. Well when we got back to the pier, there were five old guys standing in front of long wooden tables. They said they'd clean each fish for four bucks a piece. "Deal," I said. I opened my cooler and these guys reached in and went to work! Holy shit, they were cutting heads off, tails off, guts and bones were flying everywhere, and within ten minutes, they were done, and my fish was wrapped up all nice in aluminum foil. Just another one of my memories I'd thought I'd share with ya.

The moral of the story is if you're going do it, do it right! Get the greatest power tools that money can buy and that would be Milwaukee. I've been using them a long time and they never fail me. I don't just use them for scrapping, I also use them when I work on my rental properties. I've seen some guys down there with Milwaukee power tools, but not a lot. If I was in that pile with my 18 volt, Milwaukee cordless tools, I'd make no less then $500 bucks a day and that's no bullshit. The other guys down there would be lucky if I left them a brass bolt!

Now let's discuss some prices. We'll start with the screw gun, only I don't use a screw gun, I use an impact gun. I use the impact gun rather than the screw gun for one simple reason, power! The things that a screw gun doesn't have the power to drive in or back out, this thing does and then some. You can get the Milwaukee 18 Volt, impact gun with 2 lithium batteries, a battery charger, and a hard case for $169.

Now let's talk about the Milwaukee cordless. This Sawzall cuts through metal like a hot knife cuts through butter! You'll fill up bucket after bucket of precious metal with this guy on your side. You can buy the Milwaukee 18 Volt, Sawzall by itself for $139 or you can get the Sawzall with one battery, battery charger, and hard case for $239.

Let's move on to the Milwaukee 4 ½ inch cordless grinder. This guy comes in handy when you can't get the Sawzall where it needs to go. You'll buzz through bolts like they were toothpicks. You can get the Milwaukee 18 Volt, cordless grinder by itself for $119 or for $179 with a battery, a battery charger, and hard case.

You also want to keep an eye out for Milwaukee Combo Kit sales! For instance, last week, I found the 18 Volt impact gun, 18 Volt Sawzall, a work light, 2 batteries, a battery charger, and a bag, all for the price of $349. Not bad.

The reason that I say "hard case" is because you an get the tool with the hard case or canvas bag. The bag brings down the price a little bit, but not much. I like the case myself because it protects the tool.

If you want to step up your game, check out the Milwaukee Fuel line of tools, these are the tools that I buy and if the ones that I described are great, the Fuel Line is even better! Don't get me wrong, all the tools above will never let you down either, but Milwaukee Fuel tools are insane. They give you more power, a longer running time, and of course a bigger battery and a bigger price tag. Find the Milwaukee tool Rep. at any Home Depot and have him give you a demonstration (or better yet, check it out on YouTube), before you make your purchase. You'll be amazed. Either way you go, you'll certainly be the king of the scrap pile!

One last thing and then I'll rap this chapter up. If you go this route and jump in the pile, don't be intimidated by anyone. I'm down there enough to see what goes on and I see some guys get bullied right off a piece of scrap. If a loudmouth is second to get to, say an unstripped air conditioner, I've seen them barge right in and take it off of a less aggressive guy. Sure, there's enough for everyone to eat and everybody wants to get their beak wet, but you don't want to end up with the shitty end of the stick every time and let the bully get all the good scores. I watch some days and I feel like I'm at the beach watching the big, fat seagull, wasting his time chasing off all the smaller seagulls when he could be eating.

Don't get intimidated and don't back down. The first time you do, you might as well stay home because they'll run you off of every good piece of metal you find. I know it's going to be a little hard telling Big John Henry to "beat it" when he comes your way with his sledgehammer, but if you don't, your profits will be slim!

CHAPTER 17
HOSPITAL HOSPITALITY

One day, I was working on one of my rental properties and I cut my hand pretty good on an old metal miniblind while removing it. I shot over to the hospital, got a tetanus shot, and they put five stitches in the palm of my right hand. After that, I was on my way out of there.

As I walked to my truck through the parking lot, I passed by the dumpster area and because by now it's second nature, I took a glance over. There were some pretty good size filing cabinets sitting next to the dumpster and as I picked up the lid, to take a peek in the dumpster, I hear, "What the fuck are you doing, get the hell out of here loser." My head spun around like the Exorcist and the first words to fly out of my mouth were, naturally, "Fuck you!"

Here is this 300-pound, $10 an hour, fat slob security guard, who thinks that he's a cop, nearly slamming the lid down on my hand and calling me a loser. He walks around the dumpster and gets right up in my face. "Are you kidding me asshole?" I said.

"No, and if you don't leave the dumpster area, I will arrest you."

At first, I started laughing but then I couldn't resist it and my Irish temper got the best of me. "You couldn't arrest that filing cabinet."

He said a few choice words back to me and he called me short.

I'd like to have used, the old, "Yeah but if I stand on my wallet, I'll be way taller than you," line on him but seeing that I'm scrounging around through his dumpsters for scrap metal like a pauper, I don't think he would've believed me, LOL. But now, it's personal! I don't know, maybe the locking up the filing cabinet comment was a little to much for him to handle.

Rather than just going home like I planned to do (like a normal person would do), I decided to go back into the hospital and talk to someone about the scrap. The secretary pointed me into the Hospital Administrator's office and I simply introduced myself, told her that I scrapped metal, and asked her if I could have the scrap that was lying around the dumpster?

She said, "Absolutely, take it! We pay to get rid of our trash, anything that is out there, you can have it." Then she hit me with some more good news, she said that I could shoot the Security Guard! Just kidding, she said, "We also own the Assisted Living Center across the street, so you have my permission to take a look over there also."

I said, "Great, but can you give me one of your cards because you have a Security Guard out there that's locking the trash down pretty good."

She laughed and said she knew exactly who I was talking about, "Tackleberry," she called him, the crazy cop from the Police Academy movie. "I'll talk to him, don't worry, you're good," she laughed.

I've been getting metal from these two places for nine years and the guy is still a world class prick to me. I say hello to him every time I see him, just to aggravate him, and he still says nothing. I don't know, maybe the tie joke was a little too much for him to handle. Anyway, hospitals, nursing homes, and assisted living centers are great places to find scrap metal! There's always a variety and I've found everything from beds, wheelchairs, gurneys, filing cabinets, walkers, crutches, braces, and medical supplies that I don't even know what they are, other then they are metal!

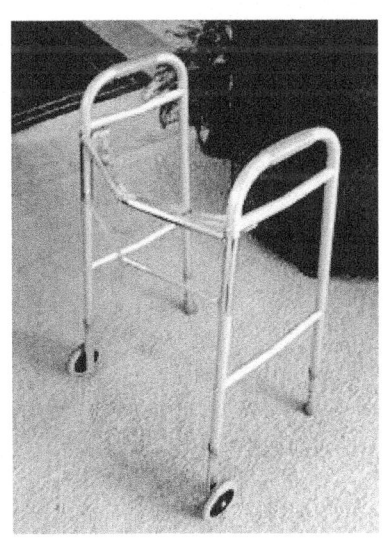

Aluminum Crutches

Metal Walkers

CHAPTER 18

APARTMENT COMPLEXES

Okay guys, this one comes from experience! If there's an apartment complex near you, make sure that you check their dumpsters. I'm not talking a house that was converted into a tri-plex or a quadruplex, I'm talking about garden style complexes that consist of 100, 200, 300 units or more. It's that *volume thing* that I talked about earlier. Once again, the more people that live somewhere, the more stuff is going to be thrown away.

When I first got out of school, I got a job as a maintenance man in a 400- unit, apartment complex. I was a metal moron back then too! When people would move out, we had to clean out their apartment. We'd

One of My First Jobs

throw out metal bedframes, metal vacuums, brass lamps, refrigerators, metal toys, toasters, microwave ovens, etc.

After the clean-out, we had to the get the unit ready for move- in. If something wasn't working and we had to replace it, this item ended up in the dumpster also. Garbage disposals, dishwashers, air conditioners, chandeliers, steel tubs, sinks, etc., all got tossed. The bigger appliances got hand trucked out of the apartment and ended up right next to the dumpster.

Here I was, an 18 year-old kid back in 1984, making 8 bucks an hour and throwing away $100 bucks in metal, a third of my pay. What an asshole! I'm glad I've finally seen the light but to be honest, I knew nothing at all about scrapping back then unless I would've cleaned up and took every stitch of metal that I could. I did then what I knew how to, now that I know, I do much

Apartment Dumpster Area

better! If anyone of you guys who bought this book for yourself, and you have a teenage son, tell him the value of metal and not to be an idiot. If he see's metal, pick it up, or better yet, tell him to tell you about it and you'll both pick it up and split it, don't let anything go to waste. Your teenage son, if he's anything like we were, is out and about all day and will see more of what's going on around town by foot, then you will by truck. It's never to early to start making money!

Now the stuff that I just described was just what we, the maintenance men, threw away. The tenants were also a gold mine! I'd see things in the dumpster area everyday such as bikes, metal tables, metal chairs, bi-fold doors, shelving, etc., enough stuff to make a good buck on. I'm going to be honest with you, because one thing I'll never do is bullshit ya. I rarely, and I mean rarely, open the dumpster lid at an apartment complex. 99% of the stuff that I want is the big, heavy items that are sitting outside of the dumpsters. Yeah, there could be a garbage disposal or a lamp in the dumpster that the maintenance man threw away, but I'm not climbing through a dumpster to get it! That's not to say you can't, I don't know how far you're willing to go for a buck but I ain't doing it.

Like I said, I want the big, heavy stuff outside the dumpster. If it's small enough to fit in the dumpster, I don't want it unless it's silver or gold! There could be treasures on the inside of the dumpster but there could also be spoiled food that stinks, roaches, or a rat that bites you on your ass. I know the saying, "The man who moves a mountain, starts by carrying away small stones," but I'll stick to the bigger stuff outside of the dumpster. The choice is yours!

CHAPTER 19

YES, YOU CAN-CAN

I have a buddy named Vern. He's pretty well to do and owns a vending company. I don't even think he knows how many machines that he has out on the street in the Tri-state area. Mac Machines, jukeboxes, snack machines, soda machines, pool tables, game rooms, etc., the list of machines goes on and on. Well when I first told him that I was scrapping metal in the morning, he laughed and said, "with all the houses you own, what the fuck are you doing scraping metal?" Believe me, if I had a nickel for everyone that asked me that, I'd have a dime. I don't know if you've

Mac Machines

ever heard the old adage about Bill Gates, but I'm going to tell it anyway.

Bill Gates makes $114 bucks, every second of the day, so it would be a bad investment for him if he saw a $100 bill laying on the ground, and it took him 2 seconds to bend over and pick it up. He would actually lose $86 bucks. Well I'm not Bill Gates and if I see a quarter laying on the ground, I'm picking it up! My point to this story is, I'm not rich enough yet where I can walk away from free money and I probably never will be!

Anyway, after I tell him how much I'm making, his ears perk up a little bit, but I still don't quite think that he believes me. He says, "I've got a ton of shit down my warehouse that I want to get rid of and I'll split the scrap money with you." Now I'm not one to go on a wild witch hunt for scrap. If I can pull my truck up and throw the scrap metal on the truck, that's what I'm looking for. I'm not spending 8 hours in someone's warehouse trying to locate enough metal to fill my truck when I can do that on any given morning. . . in an hour.

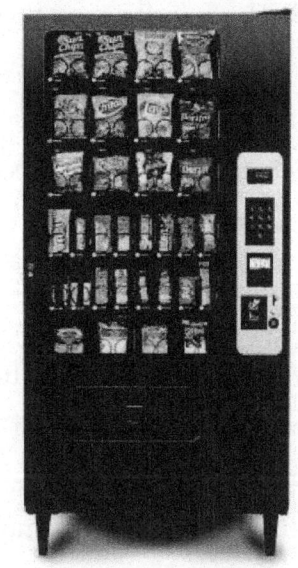

Snack Machines

So, after I decline his offer, he asks me if I'm sure? "These are some old soda and snack machines and they weigh a ton," he says. Now I'm the guy that's intrigued! "How many do you have?" He says about 30 that he'd like to get rid of, so we were on our way.

Well, we made 3 trips to the dump in four hours and we both stuck $700 apiece in our pockets. It was easy as shit loading them too because he used his forklift to put the machines onto the back of the truck. I created a monster, now Vern had scrap metal fever too!

"Mike, I know a lot of guys who pay to get rid of these things. I can put a call out to them if you want me to and we'll both clean up." Vern's warehouse is down in Delaware and to be honest, it's just a little too far and a little too much so I had to decline. I hated turning down money, but I knew that this would start cutting into my real estate time, so I had to take a pass. Like I said a million times, real estate before scrap!

I passed Rob's number on to Vern and they hook up and grab the vending machines together. Rob and Vern have become good friends too and now we all head down the casino together! Hey, you've got to have some fun and you can't take it with you. Who knows, there's a chance you might win some cash. Our motto is, "I'd risk it all for a little more." Now let me get to the "Yes you can-can," part of this chapter.

Vern has a young teenage son who is a couple of years away from graduating and starting college. Of course, Vern's going to be on the hook for the college tuition, but he told his son that if he wants spending money while he's away, he's going to earn it. Here is what Vern did.

Before I tell you what he did, I'll tell you this. Uh, I don't know if it's legal, LOL. Vern has a pick-up truck with an 8-foot bed and he simply started driving around his neighborhood the night before recycling day. This is a different day then trash day, and in some boroughs, they make you separate your aluminum cans and plastic. The cans go in one borough issued can and the plastic goes into another. He would simply grab the big, yellow, borough issued trash can and dump the cans into the back of his truck. He'd do this until the entire bed was filled with cans and it didn't take long either. He told me that he could fill the entire bed in about 20 minutes, and why not? The cans are just sitting out there in front of everybody's house, filled with aluminum. It's like shooting fish in a barrel!

Once the truck was filled with cans, he'd pull back up in his yard and sweep the cans out into his yard with a push broom. Then he would put his son to work! Vern purchased the <u>Zone 30 Gallon Can Compactor</u> for $30 off Amazon and had his son go out in the yard, crush the cans, and throw them into a 55-gallon drum. Once he'd get a couple of drums filled, he and his son would proceed to the scrap yard and here's the breakdown.

Standard Issued Borough Recycle Can

METAL MONEY

Vern would fill his truck with cans and dump them in his yard about three times per week, hitting different boroughs. That would give his son all week to work on crushing the cans and to get ready for next week's load. He figured he had his son crushing 4,000 cans per week and it's not hard. If you crush about 15 cans a minute, that comes out to about to about 900 crushed cans an hour. His son usually knocked out the whole batch in about four to four and a half hours a week. Now here's the cash breakdowns.

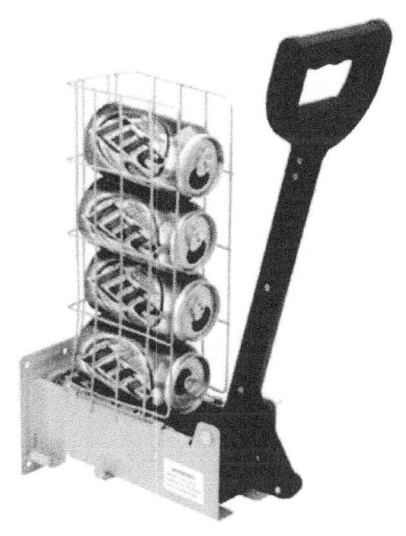

Can Crusher

Vern's Son's College Money!

Right now (2019), the price for aluminum cans is 48 cents per pound. A can weighs a half an ounce, so you would need 32 cans to equal a pound. That breaks down to each individual can being worth 1.5 cents. Vern collects 4,000 cans so let's do the math (my God, this sounds like one of those long, drawn out, fifth grade math questions I used to get)!

4,000 Cans	$60 Per Week
X .015 Cents	X 52 Weeks
= $60	= 3,120 A Year!

Right now, Vern's son is 16 years old and they've been collecting cans for two years. He has just over $6,500 saved already for college! In two more years, he'll hit the $13,000 mark and he'll be the richest kid on the Penn State campus, just from crushing cans for a couple hours a week.

One thing that Vern mentioned to me, that might be useful to you if you have the room for it, is that you can hoard the cans. He'll keep filling up the 55- gallon drums until the price of aluminum goes up. If aluminum is up high and then takes a slight dip, he gets rid of it before the price of aluminum sinks. Like I always say, timing is everything in life.

Another thing that I'll tell you is that he and his son look forward to cashing the scrap in at the yard, it's become a bonding experience. His son gets excited to see what kid of money he's made, and it gives him a little sense of how hard work can pay off. Then, they go out to breakfast together and make a full morning out of it. Look what I started, see how great a guy I am, LOL.

The final thing that I want to talk about is that *illegal* thing that I talked about in the beginning of the chapter. I know that a lot of these townships don't want you to take their recyclables (as if they're really theirs), but I've never, ever heard of anyone getting arrested for it. I'm sure that I will get an email from a couple of people who have been, or know someone who has been, arrested for taking the cans from somebody's trash but I honestly don't know of anyone in the can for stealing cans! Be careful and scrap at your own risk!

CHAPTER 20

BUILDING A GOOD ROUTE

What started out as a fun way to kill a couple hours in the morning and make a couple extra bucks, has led to a lot of customers wanting me to stop by their businesses and pick up their scrap metal. I only do this for twenty or so hours a week but if I wasn't into being a Section 8 landlord, I could do this for 60 hours a week and make a lot more money driving around and picking up scrap.

I only do what I want to do at this point in my life and believe me, I turn down way more work then I accept, which you don't have to. If someone calls with a one time pick-up, unless it's a huge score, I usually turn it down. If they tell me I can come by every week and fill my truck with scrap, I'll add it to my route. Like rent money, it's that residual money that I seek!

I'll also replace bad stops with good stops. For instance, when the woman from the hospital told me that I can take her scrap and the nursing home's scrap, I dumped a concrete plant that was giving me their steel forms and rebar. The steel forms were nice, but they were always attached to huge chunks of concrete that had to be broken and smashed loose from the forms unless the scrapyard guy would yell at me like I was trying to cheat him on the weight, because the concrete added to the weight of metal. I've read dozens of books about heroes and crooks and I've learned much from both of their styles, trying to add 20 pounds of concrete at a nickel a pound? I think I'd rather try to my luck at robbing banks. Anyway, it was a big pain in the ass so adios-amigos to the concrete plant.

Residual income is how to build a good route! People that count on you every week, or month, to come by and pick up their stuff, and you can count on it being there. That's another reason I won't and don't like to go into people's homes to collect scrap. After you leave, and they tell you not to let the door hit'cha where the good lord split'cha, you'll never see or hear from them again. It's just not worth it to me.

Then again, who the hell am I? What's not worth it to me, may be worth it to you! What I'm trying to tell you in this chapter is to maximize. If you work a fulltime job and have limited time to do this, say 12 hours a week, then god damn it, make sure that you are jamming in your best and most profitable stops during these 12 hours!

If I only had 12 hours a week, I'd definitely still do my Southwest Philly morning run (9 hours), Friday night with Ray at the machine shop (2 hours), and I'd do my Muffler Shop pick-up (1hour). And guess what, I'd still make a nice buck.

CHAPTER 21

WHAT YOU WILL NEED TO GET STARTED

Simple, I can sum this entire chapter up with one word, a truck! Big or small, it doesn't matter, but of course, the bigger the truck that you have, the easier and larger appliances you'll be able to fit on it. I see a lot of guys at the scrapyard with the smaller, 6- foot beds, making a good buck but most guys have the 8- foot bed, a dump truck, or a stake body, and they have it down to a science!

An 8 Foot Bed Pick Up Truck Will Work Fine

You can fit 2,000 pounds of scrap into a 1- ton pickup like the Ford F 250 and if scrap is going for 6 cents a pound, you just made $120 bucks. It doesn't take long to fill up a pickup truck with scrap metal. A couple heavy items and you're there. Me, I have a stake body that is supposed to hold 5,000 pounds but I overload it all the time and I see no sag in the suspension. Using that scenario of 6 cents a pound, I'd get $300 for a full load. Plus, I don't have to keep burning gas going back and forth to dump it, I just keep motoring along until it's filled.

I got my truck for $5,500 bucks, 18 years ago, and I still use it today. I don't have to pull anything off it because it dumps. I just press a button and the scrap easily slides right off the truck. I don't have to worry about cutting my hand, stepping on a nail, or stubbing my toe on an appliance. It's the best $5,500 I ever spent in my life!

I've seen a good amount of people come to the scrapyard in a car. I automatically peg that guy for a drug addict or a jerk-off, excuse my French. They fill the trunk and backseat with so much metal that the springs on the car can't take it, and the trunk is damn near dragging on the ground. It's like trying to get 10 pounds of shit into a 5 pound bag.

This is a Huge No No!

Then, once they weigh in, they have to pull one metal item at a time, out of their trunk and backseat. I collect two large loads, get them unloaded, and cash my tickets before they can get one load done and that's no bullshit. Don't be *"that guy."*

You can get a good, used truck for $3,000 or less. It doesn't have to be pretty, it can be old and ugly, it doesn't make a difference, as long as it runs well. All you're doing is scrapping with it and it's not going to be your family vehicle. I will tell you this, every load that you dump, put a little in savings toward a stake body, preferably one that dumps. The money you'll start pulling down with a bigger truck is incredible!

The next thing I'll tell you that would be great to have. . . but you don't need it. It'll make quick work of large appliances, like refrigerators and washers, and it will also save you future back problems. The item that I'm talking about is, of course, a hand truck. Not just any hand truck, but a Magliner! Now, I've used the cheaper hand trucks and they suck. When you get a heavy appliance on a smaller, non-sturdy hand truck, you don't know what they're going to do, they're to unpredictable. Sometimes they tip sideways, sometimes when you lean them back, the refrigerator comes down on top of you, the strap always rips, and the tires always go flat. There is nothing worse than relying on a piece of shit, human or machine!

You won't get that with a Magliner! Buy one and you'll have it for life. I like the Magliner Convertible, it converts into several different positions that sometime or another, will be useful to you. They're a little pricey, but good ain't cheap and cheap ain't good! I paid $440 for mine but you can get it for less. I didn't want the pneumatic wheels on mine, which take air. Instead, I upgraded to the solid foam filled wheels which never go flat and give you a smooth ride. You can also upgrade to a cheaper solid rubber tire which also will never go flat, but the tires are skinnier, and you won't get that smooth ride when hauling an appliance down the street. Both are good though. They also sell a hand truck that is not a convertible for around $250, it'll also get the job done for you.

Magliner Convertible

The last thing that you don't need, but would be helpful to have, are the same tools that I spoke about in Chapter 16, Tools Needed for Picking off the Pile. These same three cordless power tools, a screw gun, a Sawzall, and a grinder will really make your life easy and speed up a ton of removals. You never know when you're going to have to cut a refrigerator door off, grind out a bolt, or remove a bracket to get to a jackpot of brass!

Like I said in chapter 16, I only use Milwaukee tools and I think they are the greatest! Believe me, I'm talking from experience here. I was a big DeWalt guy for years and years. In fact, I tried Milwaukee years ago, but their tools didn't hold up and I continued to use DeWalt. One day I was in Home Depot and the Milwaukee Rep. told me everything about how they changed everything around and urged me to give them a shot, so I did. It was the best decision, tool wise, that I ever made. Their tools are so innovative, and sturdy built that they will outlast, and out- perform DeWalt on any given day of the week. Their battery charge lasts forever, which is what I like the best. I don't get paid a nickel to plug Milwaukee tools but believe me, you'll thank me after purchasing one.

That's really the only thing that you'll need in this business. If you want to throw in a tape measure to make sure things fit through the door, knock yourself out. Any other business that you want to get involved in, I guarantee, you will have insane start-up money needed. Not scrapping! Get a truck, find the scrap, make the money. It's pretty cut and dry when you break it down like that.

I know that in most "how to" books, they tell you in the first chapter or two, what you'll need to get involved in the business. I purposely waited to put what you need to get started in the back of my book and I'll tell you why. I didn't want to discourage anyone from thinking that there was going to be a laundry list of things you'll need. A truck, some motivation, and common sense can go a long way in this business!

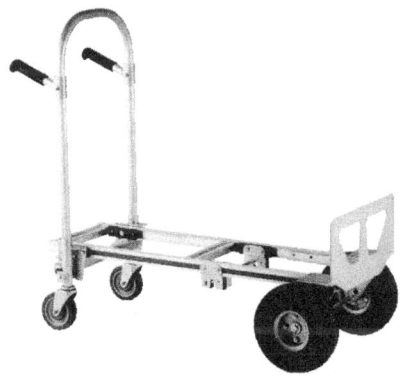

Converts to Different Positions

CHAPTER 22

CRAIGSLIST – LET GO – MARKETPLACE

This chapter may well be the shortest chapter that I have ever written in my life. I never have collected metal like this, and I don't intend on it, but Rob does, and he said I should write about it, so I'll throw it in as a bonus.

Rob told me that when he gets a little slow sometimes, he'll jump on the internet to locate scrap metal. He'll go on any of the above mentioned, sites (there's probably hundreds more), and look up "free stuff." He will comb down the lists and if he finds something worth it's weight to go pick up, he'll do it.

He told me that he has had some pretty good scores with old aluminum windows, screen doors, heavy machinery, tools, exercise equipment, etc. He'll try to map out 6 or 7 stops on his run. He tries to keep them somewhat in the same area so that he's not burning a ton of gas and the trip is worthwhile.

One thing that he says he never does, believe it or not, is to tell the donor that he is going to scrap whatever it is they are giving him. He told me that a lot of people would get insulted and pissed at him if he said that he was taking it to the scrapyard. Now, he tells them that whatever it is they are giving him, is really going to help him out. They feel good about themselves for helping, Rob's glad that he got the metal, and then it's straight to the scrapyard!

If you are going to score metal this way, take the magnet with your scrap name off the side of your truck for the day. If it's painted on there, unless you get inventive, you're screwed!

CHAPTER 23

MIKE'S FINAL THOUGHT'S

Well folks, that's just about going to do it. How did it get so late so soon? Like I say in all my Section 8 Real Estate books, either write things worthy of reading, or do things worthy of writing and I believe I have done both! I've written a book that I hope will help you make some extra cash scrapping metal, and I've lived the life of a part time scrapper. I sincerely hope that you enjoyed the book!

Throughout this book, I couldn't stress enough that I do this hustle *part time*, and I make great money, probably more money than some people who work a 40- hour week, and I mean that with no disrespect. But just think of the money that you could make if you jump into this business fulltime, the potential is unlimited!

I'm being 100% honest when I tell you that I turn down way more work then I accept, and if you think about it, that makes sense. Only 30% of all the metal that is made every day, is being recycled. What that means is that the other 70% is sooner or later going to turn up on somebody's sidewalk and hopefully, you're there to grab it (unless it ends up in Southwest Philly, keep your paws off it)!

I don't treat my scrap business, or the 20 hours that I put into it a week, like it's a business at all, and that's my fault. I try to keep it light and keep it fun. I never let it stress me out at all. My stress starts at 8 o'clock when I start arguing with tenants, contractors, and inspectors (that's another book). I came up with the number, "2,000 a month" because I believe you can easily do it. I don't have a formula and I don't think I need one, 2 grand is very doable! I just believe that if you're not lazy, this is a legitimate number that you can build up to in your spare time. If I'm doing 6 or 7 grand a month part time, then you should be able to do two grand. It's not hard, the scrap is out there, and I just told you where to start looking for it.

I guarantee you (I know, I do a lot of guaranteeing don't I), most of you who are reading this book are willing to go further than me, and that really shouldn't be hard. Here are the top 10 reasons why you should be able to do better than me at this business:

1. I want to have fun, not kill myself.
2. I don't want to go into people's homes, even if they're sitting on a copper gold mine.
3. I don't want to lift a dumpster lid or climb through a dumpster that has trash in it, but more importantly, possibly has metal in it.
4. I don't want to strip or separate my metal and increase my profits.
5. I won't advertise, even on free sites.

6. If it's below 25 degrees, I ain't goin' out, scrapping's cancelled.
7. I don't think there's enough money in sheet metal. $30 bucks an hour, not enough, and I cry that it hurts my feet to stomp it down.
8. I won't go out a week before or after Christmas. I'd rather eat and drink eggnog.
9. Sometimes when it rains, I'll pay my other worker to help Rob throw things on the truck, while I stay dry in the truck and listen to the radio.
10. I turn down jobs that are more then five miles from my house, just because I don't feel like getting stuck in traffic.

I could probably think of another 10 reasons why you should be able to make more than me, but I don't want to embarrass myself anymore! If you can't beat my scrap work ethic and make $2,000 a month, then you're not doing something right. Wow! I didn't realize how light I take this business until I wrote those ten things down, LOL.

Truthfully, I'm not afraid to get my hands dirty to make a buck and I never have been. When I was an 8 year-old kid, I heard my late Uncle Harry say, "I'd shovel shit all day if the price was right," and it stuck with me all my life. In my real estate world, I'm the hardest working Landlord that you'll ever meet, period! I do 90% of the work on my properties, swing deals all day long, deal with tenants and contractors all day, scrap and hunt metal before and after work, and when I get home, I write books!

There are other landlords that don't own 10% of what I own, who hire management companies and don't lift a finger or even get dirty.

Me, I come home from work filthy and I love it, it keeps me young! I don't mean to be pumping my own tires up here but after shaming myself with that "10 reasons" stunt, I had to redeem myself with you guys, LOL!

I didn't mean to get sidetracked with real estate so let's get back to Scrap Metal (it's that lose bolt I tell ya, that damn loose bolt). Okay, listen, this is the cheapest business to get into, and if you have a truck, you're already 99% of the way there! Everything that you pick up and throw into the back of your truck is going to be pure profit. What other business in the world can say that? None!

Some people who need a little extra cash, want to do crazy stuff, like go to yard sales or flea markets and buy stuff to sell on Amazon or Ebay. Screw that! Half the time, they get stuck with half the stuff that they buy, and they lose money because they can't get rid of it. Now think about scrap metal. You always have a buyer in place, plenty of them! No matter how much metal that you collect, you'll be able to get rid of every shred of it, every single time, any given day.

It's beautiful and I wish that I would have been doing it earlier in my life. I still have nightmares about some of the Metal Money that I left on the table or gave away! Use this book as a guide and give it a go with a scrap business and I promise you this, you'll be a "scrapper" for life!

CHAPTER 24

WRAPPING IT UP!

Hey guys, I sincerely want to thank you for purchasing my book and I hope that you enjoyed it. I also hope that you got your money's worth and that you use these tips to make hundreds of thousands of dollars in the future! If I got you interested or motivated, maybe that's the spark that you needed to get things rolling. The easiest way to get started is to quit talking and start doing!

Let me tell you a little bit about myself. I love to make money scrapping metal and I love being a Section 8 Landlord, but what I really, really love to do is write! I know, it sounds weird right? The thing that I make the least amount of money from is the thing that I like to do the most. It figures, LOL. It really means a lot to me when somebody thoroughly enjoys one of my books and hates to see it come to an end. Whether I taught you a thing or two, made you laugh once or twice, or hopefully just let you block the world out and escape for a couple hours after a hectic workday, I hope the cover price was worth it to you!

I enjoy living life and striking up conversations with total strangers, that's how I learned 90% of the things that I learned in life. I was never shy, never afraid to ask questions, and never acted like I was better or smarter than anyone else just because I've got a little bit of money. I enjoy learning from people and the more of a character you are, usually, the more I like to talk to you!

Let me tell you where I meet a ton of characters, at the scrapyard! I've met more characters at the scrapyard then there are characters walking around in Disney Land and Disney World combined. Guy's that are a little rough on the outside, but nice enough on the inside to share their knowledge and advice with me, and that's where I came up with the idea for my next book!

Like I said, I've become friendly with a ton of guys down at the scrapyard. I picked out and wrote a list of 25 or 30 guys that I just want to sit down with and talk about scrapping. These are the guys that I was telling you about, the guys that know everything there is to know about scrapping! They know every type of metal, what's the easiest way to get it, and when's the best time to sell it.

I want it all and I'm going to ask every single one of them the same three questions. Tell me a tip that you can share with a novice that will instantly increase their profit margin? Tell me a place where someone would never think to find scrap? And finally, tell me your craziest or funniest scrap metal story. I may have to bribe a couple of them with lunch from the hotdog cart up the street, but I'll get'em to talk, that I'm sure of.

I've already been picking some of their brains and telling them that I'm writing a book about scrapping. One smartass already said to me, "Write everything that you know, that should leave you with a lot of free time," LOL, like I said, they're characters! Another guy shared with me a story about seeing a lawnmower out front of someone's house. He thought it was trash, threw it onto his truck, and the homeowner came running out of the back yard with an ax in his hand and chased him up the street, so this should prove interesting none the less!

I've already started the book. It's going to be called, "Metal Money Maniacs," so keep an eye out for it. One last thing before I go, if you guys enjoyed this book, please make sure that you give me a review on Amazon or wherever you read it, it helps. Also, if I piqued your interest a tad about getting involved in Section 8 Rentals, you can check out my website at www.section8bible.com or check out my Section 8 Bible books on Amazon. You may find other books on Section 8 real estate, but I forgot more than the other guys know about how to make money in this industry. They'll take your money, I'll make you rich! Thanks again for your purchase and happy scrapping. Now go make a fortune!

MIKE MCLEAN

Check out my books on how to make money with Section 8 rental properties!

www.section8bible.com

Other real estate books will take your money.

I'll make you rich!

Other books by this author:
Section 8 Bible: How to Invest in Low-Income Housing
Section 8 Bible Volume 2
Section 8 Bible Volume 3
Section 8 Secrets: Get Housing Assistance Faster